OVERCOMING THE SPIRIT OF NARCISSISM

OVERCOMING THE SPIRIT OF NARCISSISM

Breaking the destructive patterns of self-idolatry and self-exaltation

PATRICIA KING

Published by XP Publishing
A department of Christian Services Association
P.O. Box 1017, Maricopa, Arizona 85139
www.XPpublishing.com

ISBN-13: 978-1-936101-10-8

ISBN-10: 1-936101-10-6

Printed in Canada. For worldwide distribution.

Dedicated to

All our ministry team at XP

who embrace the Kingdom values of

humility, servanthood, faith and selfless love...

yes, **LOVE.**

Table of Contents

FOREWORD

by ***Patricia King***

I sometimes like watching crime shows that reveal the conquering of lawlessness and the establishment of justice. Some episodes I've watched portray situations where a narcissistic sociopath is pursued, arrested, tried, convicted and sentenced.

I did not know too much about narcissism so I decided to engage in a study, out of curiosity. Through my research I discovered that narcissism is not confined to sociopathic murderers but can also manifest through people who have never broken civil or federal laws. I found that there are mild and severe symptoms, but all of it is fueled with self-exaltation, pride, self-absorption and self-focus.

During my season of investigation, information regarding narcissistic behavior seemed to be heralded in news headlines and broadcasts, in books and internet articles on a regular basis. Everywhere I looked it was in my face. In reviewing certain scenarios I was aware of in the church, I could see patterns and symptoms of this disorder running rampant and not being identified, confronted or conquered. I saw people influenced at home, in the work place, in schools and in local churches. I saw both men and women plagued and bound by this.

Criminology, sociology and psychology professors around the world are teaching students about this disorder, as it is a growing problem today. The more I researched, the more I realized that the world had few solutions and very little hope. But what does the Bible say? What does God say?

In the following pages I will attempt to briefly unpack some revelation regarding narcissism: what it is and how to overcome it. With Christ all things are possible.

Love is the weapon and the force that will take out this destructive entity. Love – pure, selfless love is our hope and our victory!

CHAPTER ONE

What Is Narcissism?

Narcissism – the Myth

The word *narcissism* comes from the Greek myth of Narcissus, who was a very attractive young man, loved and admired by many. He was renowned for his beauty and was greatly favored, attracting attention wherever he went and in whatever he did. In various versions of the myth, he is portrayed as exceptionally cruel, in that he eventually despised and rejected those who loved him and gave their full attention and heart to him. Narcissus invited the adoration and praise given him by all, but he himself loved no one and never reciprocated the love given to him. In his own eyes, there was no one equal to him or truly worthy of him.

The myth portrays the destructive patterns and cycles of self-admiration. Narcissus was unable to love or connect with anyone outside himself, and the rejection he gave to others severely hurt those who loved him.

In the myth, Echo (a wood nymph who because of a curse could only repeat words that were spoken to her) fell deeply in love with Narcissus and longed to be noticed and adored by him. The dream of her heart was for Narcissus to take notice of her, claiming her as his own forever. In order to gain his affection, she would go to any length to please and serve him.

One day while in the woods, Narcissus called out to her, inviting her to join him. Echo was delighted. Narcissus had noticed her and called her to himself! Finally her inner longings were being realized. She ran towards him and threw herself upon him. She wholeheartedly gave herself to him, but in return Narcissus cruelly rejected her and threw her to the ground with repulsion and walked away.

Echo left the woods devastated, ashamed, brokenhearted and crushed in spirit. She lived alone in the mountain ranges for the rest of her days. Daily she longed and pined for a love that would never be returned. She finally died of grief and loneliness, and her body became one with the mountain stone. All that was left was her voice that echoed what others spoke.

Narcissus continued to attract the attention and love of many nymphs. He would entertain them for a season, receiving their attention and adoration, and then would ultimately reject each one. The gods disliked the way he was treating others and as a result cursed him forever. They wanted him to know what it felt like to love and never be loved in return.

One day, while walking in the forest he came upon a small lake, as smooth as glass. As he gazed into the pool, he saw a beautiful image of himself, although he did not recognize his own reflection. He was captivated by the image he saw. Never had he felt such personal attraction! Never had he felt love like this. As he bent down to kiss the vision, he noticed that the reflection copied his actions. This intensified his intrigue and emotional longings. He had finally found someone who was one with him that he could truly admire and love! He reached into the reflection to draw the image to himself, thinking it was a water spirit. As he touched the water, the reflection disappeared. He was distraught and panicked, wondering where his love had gone. When the water became calm, the reflection returned. He cried out to the reflection, "Oh beautiful one, where did you go? Why did you leave me?"

He once more reached out to touch the one he loved. As his hands touched the water, the image disappeared again. He became fearful and no longer wanted to touch the water, as he did not want the one he longed for to leave him. He lay on the bank of the pool gazing into the eyes of the reflection but was unable to connect. He pined by the hour and refused to eat or drink. At first, many came around to comfort and encourage. Others offered counsel to help him overcome, but he rejected each one. After many days and numerous failed attempts they all left him. As time went on he withered away, becoming emaciated and losing his beauty. He eventually died all alone in severe grief and loneliness on the banks of the pond. His body disappeared and a flower now known as the narcissus (a species of daffodil) grew in its place.

The story of Echo and Narcissus portrays the deception, trap and ultimate tragedy and destruction of self-idolatry. It also reveals the pain and grief of those who love someone who cannot, or will not, reciprocate that love.

Lucifer the Ultimate Narcissist

Lucifer was the ultimate narcissist and ultimate enemy to God and His Kingdom. He was the anointed covering cherub, created the most beautiful being in heaven and given a position of influence and honor (see Ezekiel 28:14). He lived in a perfect environment of love, blessing, purity and glory, yet he chose to sin and he invited the worship and focus of all unto himself. He exalted himself above God and all He created. Lucifer became completely self-absorbed, self-focused, self-exalting and self-fulfilling – the main characteristics of narcissism. A clear profile of narcissism is evidenced in the scriptural study of the behavior and actions of Lucifer.

Isaiah 14:13-14 gives us a glimpse into Lucifer's exalted heart, "But you said in your heart, 'I will ascend to heaven; I will raise my throne above the stars of God, and I will sit on the mount of assembly in the recesses of the north. I will ascend above the heights of the clouds; I will make myself like the Most High.' "

In Ezekiel 28:12-17 the Scripture further confirms that Lucifer, the anointed covering cherub, was created the most beautiful, most gifted and most blessed of all, yet he chose to arrogantly exalt himself above God.

> "[12]Thus says the Lord God, 'You had the seal of perfection, full of wisdom and perfect in beauty. [13]You were in Eden, the garden of God; every precious stone was your covering: the ruby, the topaz and the diamond; the beryl, the onyx and the jasper; the lapis lazuli, the turquoise and the emerald; and the gold, the workmanship of your settings and sockets, was in you. On the day that you were created they were prepared. [14]You were the anointed cherub who covers, and I placed you there. You were on the holy mountain of God; you walked in the midst of the stones of fire. [15]You were blameless in your ways from the day you were created until unrighteousness was found in you. [16]By the abundance of your trade you were internally filled with violence, and you sinned; therefore I have cast you as profane from

the mountain of God. And I have destroyed you, O covering cherub, from the midst of the stones of fire. [17]Your heart was lifted up because of your beauty; you corrupted your wisdom by reason of your splendor. I cast you to the ground; I put you before kings, that they may see you.'"

The Disorder and the Demon

Narcissistic Personality Disorder (NPD) is the name given to a behavioral and social disorder based on the symptoms, effects and consequences of extreme self-focus and self-idolatry. It involves egotistical pursuits, offering self-gratification, dominance and ambition to the exclusion of others. The name of the disorder is taken from the previously mentioned Greek myth of Narcissus and Echo.

The Mayo Clinic staff gives the following description: "Narcissism is a disorder in which people have an inflated sense of their own importance and a deep need for admiration. Those with Narcissistic Personality Disorder believe that they're superior to others and have little regard for other people's feelings. But behind this 'mask' of ultra-confidence lies a fragile self-esteem, vulnerable to the slightest criticism."

Often, there can be a demonic control associated with the disorder, as well. Whenever an individual "creates a landing strip" through sin, they are open for demonic oppression. As I shared earlier, Satan, once a beautiful angel named Lucifer, is now fallen from his heavenly position and is God's archenemy for all time. He prowls around like a roaring lion, looking for someone to devour. He is looking for those who will submit to him that he might rule over them, controlling them with his deception and rebellion and conforming them unto his likeness.

Romans 6:16 teaches us that, "When you present yourselves to someone as slaves for obedience, you are slaves of the one whom you obey, either of sin resulting in death, or of obedience resulting in righteousness." When you give yourself to sin, you create a landing strip for the enemy, granting him legal license to control in the areas opened to him. Sin is dangerous. The enemy is watching to find those points of legal access so that he might steal, kill and destroy (see John 10:10).

Demons can control a person who is operating in narcissistic behavior. Through the gift of the discerning of spirits (1 Corinthians 12:10), we can identify their demonic control as "spirits of narcissism." We are to expose, identify and annihilate their ungodly assignments through discernment, true repentance and the execution of the power of the name of Jesus. Spirits of narcissism jump on the landing strip of sin and deception. In Christ, we have power over all the power of the enemy, and nothing will injure us (Luke 10:19). We are well able to overcome any assignment of the enemy through Christ.

The Nature of Deception

When you are deceived you do not know it; that is the nature of it. Deception is different from rebellion. If you were to rebel, you would know what is right yet deliberately choose to do what is wrong. When deceived, you actually believe you are right. Deception creates blind spots in your perception so that you cannot actually see the truth. What you believe feels like the truth when you are deceived. Narcissism is rooted in deception. In the myth, when Narcissus looked into the reflection he actually believed with full conviction that it was a true being he could love. It was not true, so he died believing the lie. This is the nature of deception.

The best safeguard against deception is a good accountability team around you. People who love you enough to speak the truth to you are great gifts. Narcissus had those around him who tried to comfort him but not those who spoke the truth. I love accountability. I listen and submit to the input from my accountability relationships. This is a safeguard against deception. Unfortunately, I know some who have put accountability teams around them but when confrontation came, they dissolved the members who disagreed with them. They then surrounded themselves with "yes men."

The outcome was disastrous as they continued to grow in deception rather than truth. They put the original team around them for appearance sake only and not for functionality. In such cases, others in their sphere of influence are affected and infected by the deception also. This type of action in response to confrontation is actually a symptom of a spirit of narcissism at work, and it potentially fuels the spirit's influence in addition to increasing its hold on those who succumb to its deception.

CHAPTER TWO

THE SYMPTOMS, THE FRUIT AND THE BEHAVIOR

How can you discern the presence of narcissism? Jesus taught, "You will know them by their fruits" (Matthew 7:16). In addition to operating in the gift of the discerning of spirits, you can determine narcissistic behavior by observing the symptoms and the fruit.

SYMPTOMS OF NARCISSISM

Those affected by narcissistic behavior will often manifest a number or all of the following symptoms:

1. Pride and arrogance
2. Brag on their achievements
3. Blame others for their shortcomings
4. Focus on outward physical and material appearances
5. Focus on an increase of material possessions; materialistic

6. Look for associations that make them "look good" or who will benefit their agendas and progress
7. Self-focused, self-absorbed, self-admiration, self-gratification, selfish ambition
8. Manipulate in order to achieve their plans and fulfill their agendas
9. Motivated to engage in relationships only for self-gratification
10. Look for attention, esteem and honor from others towards them
11. Make decisions based on their personal benefit and not for the sake of others
12. Exploit people, their gifts and sphere of influence in order to advance their own selfish purposes and gain
13. Will be kind and generous only if it ultimately benefits them
14. Use charm to get their way – often very charismatic
15. Are never satisfied
16. Blinded to their shortcomings and are not usually willing to have others point out faults even if the confrontation is delivered in a loving way

17. Lack empathy
18. Shallow values
19. Celebrity mindset (love the limelight and special attention as a VIP)
20. Often have addictive and compulsive disorders
21. Aggression and angry outbursts, especially when confronted or opposed
22. Prone to lies, exaggerations and fabrications
23. Blame and shame shifts when confronted or convicted; lack of true conviction
24. Do not care about the effect of their choices on others as long as it is beneficial for them
25. Obsessed with fantasies of unlimited success
26. Require excessive praise, admiration and adulation
27. Demand immediate compliance to their orders, instructions, expectations and directions
28. Feel grandiose and self-important
29. Listen to what others have to say only if they mirror their viewpoints
30. Believe the only great ideas are their own
31. Underestimate challenges facing them and pretend to be a "know-it-all"

32. Cannot forget a wrong done to them and may be prone to seek revenge
33. May have a condescending or belittling attitude toward their employees
34. Believe they are the exception to any rules that do not support their agenda

To some, narcissists may seem like they have great confidence or high self-esteem. Unfortunately, those with narcissistic personality disorder cross the border of healthy confidence and self-esteem into thinking so highly of themselves that they put themselves on pedestals. People who have healthy confidence and self-esteem don't value themselves more than they value others. Jesus said to be great in the Kingdom of God was to be least of all. A true heart of a servant is to lift up others, and God promises to lift us up if we do. We do not have to do our own lifting up!

> Pride goes before destruction, and a haughty spirit before stumbling (Proverbs 16:18).

> Sitting down, He called the twelve and said to them, "If anyone wants to be first, he shall be last of all and servant of all" (Mark 9:35).

> "Whoever then humbles himself as this child, he is the greatest in the kingdom of heaven" (Matthew 18:4).

The Fruit of Narcissism

The following are some examples of possible fruit found in those bound by narcissism:

1. Broken relationships and covenants
2. Rejection
3. Division in homes, workplaces, spheres of influence, relationships and church
4. Mental illness – breakdowns, sociopathic behavior in severe cases
5. Criminal activity
6. Causes emotional abuse

Narcissistic Behavior

Narcissism can be found anywhere – in the home, the workplace, in schools and yes, even in the church. The following examples are scenarios that reveal narcissistic behavior in different environments.

Brandon

Brandon, a 17-year-old, broke into his grandmother's home, stealing her gold coin collection appraised at approximately $20,000. Immediately after the theft, he sold it at a pawn shop for $1,500 cash.

His parents and grandmother reported the crime and were called to the local police station when the law enforcement officers made the arrest. They were shocked, perplexed, shaken and deeply hurt to find that their own son and grandson had violated and betrayed them in this way. His mother, weeping uncontrollably, asked, "Why? Why? I can't believe that you stole from your own grandmother! Why?"

Brandon responded with indignation, "I overheard you guys last week when you read her will at the house. The b__ch left everything to you, Dad, Uncle Terry and Aunt Sue. She left nothing to me. I didn't steal; I just took what was mine. I deserve it. It was not right for her to leave me out of the will, and if she was going to act like that, then I was going for what was rightfully mine. What does it matter to the b__ch, anyway? She's not going to be around that much longer, and a few coins aren't going to make a difference."

Through the process, the parents further discovered that Brandon was using drugs. When confronted, he simply responded, "I deserve to feel good." There was no remorse. He was upset about being caught and demanded seasoned legal support to get him off the charges, as he felt he did not deserve the discomfort of confinement.

Brandon, although raised in a loving home, was self-absorbed and could not reciprocate that love. His world was all about him. A spirit of narcissism fueled Brandon's self-idolatry and sociopathic behavior.

Megan

Megan was the only daughter and the youngest child in a family of four children. Her parents had wanted a girl from the time they were expecting their second child. When Megan was born, she was the center of attention in the home. The "princess" learned how to charm her parents and her brothers at an early age. She received a great deal of affirmation and attention in the home. She could do no wrong in the eyes of her family, and the sun rose and set upon her. As a result, she became very self-focused and absorbed. Some days she would change her clothes three times in order to hear her family tell her how great she looked. She loved the attention, and if they were not giving it to her she would find a way to get it.

When Megan went to school she hit a crisis. She discovered quickly that in the schoolyard she was not the center of attention like she was in her home. This was the beginning of learning deceptive, attention-getting behavior. She placed demands on her parents for new clothes because she found that when she donned a new, trendy outfit she would receive extra attention from the other girls coveting her apparel. She liked being envied. She was obsessed with her appearance by the fifth grade, and stood in front of a mirror for long periods of time admiring herself. She bought glamour books by the rack and determined to keep up with the latest fashions.

She started to physically develop as a woman in the seventh grade and became obsessed with the attention of boys. She made sure she got their admiration and learned seductive ways to attract them. From adolescence, she loved the attention of the opposite sex but never wanted to commit to any. All of her relationships were short-lived, as they all fell short of meeting her needs. She would dump one and go to the next.

At 16 years of age she asked her parents for breast implant surgery for her birthday present. They discouraged her, but promised that if she still wanted the surgery at age 21, they would give it to her as a special birthday present. By the time she was 25 years of age she had gone through numerous cosmetic surgeries, treatments, breast implants, nose reconstruction and cheek reconstruction. She was also obsessed with diet and exercise and suffered from a shopping addiction. Megan was enamored with her appearance. She lived to hear the approval of others. She lived to be the center of attention.

Megan became competitive and successful in her career as a sales person for a cosmetic company. She learned to aggressively pursue business connections that would further her career. She was not genuinely interested in meeting her clients, but made it appear that way so she could get what she wanted from them. She built convenient business connections in order to climb the corporate ladder and did not care about stepping on anyone's toes to get what she wanted. Every choice in life was about what benefited her personally.

One evening she was watching a television feature on a particular Hollywood celebrity that she envied. The feature highlighted the generosity of the actress and boasted on her compassionate and giving heart. The program host interviewed young admirers of this actress who were deeply touched by this aspect of her character. One girl cried out as the camera filmed her, "She has so much love!" She then hysterically screamed, "She is the best, she is the best!"

The very next day after viewing the program, Megan made a large contribution to a charity and let everyone know about it. She privately admitted to some friends that she did not have a heart for the needy at all but the public display of her generosity gave her favor with some influential people in her field. She was using her ostentatious act of benevolence for personal leverage. Her motive in publicly demonstrating generosity was to receive attention and benefit from her good works. If the benevolent deed did not give opportunity for personal gratification, then she would not have done it. Later she openly and shamelessly admitted to this.

She married at 29 years of age and divorced her husband within 18 months because he did not have the means to treat her as she felt she deserved.

A spirit of narcissism possessed Megan.

Brian

Brian grew up in a very tumultuous home. Every day there were fights between his parents. Anger and rage were the order of the day in his household. Both his parents were addicted to drugs and alcohol. His father would leave the home for months at a time. This would be repeated a number of times in any given year and when Brian was five years old, his father left for good. His mother neglected him due to her addictions, and he was eventually removed from his home and placed in foster care.

Brian got involved with a group of rebels in school and entered a life of crime and addiction at an early age. He was sentenced to juvenile detention for the first time at age 14 and was in and out of detention over the next number of years due to his developing life of crime. While institutionalized, he learned to be a master liar and manipulator.

Years later he openly admitted to the skillful lies he regularly communicated, and boasted to many on how he had learned to get his way with any guard or counselor in the system.

At age 21 he had a genuine spiritual encounter that transformed his life. He enjoyed true love and care for the first time in his existence. Jesus Christ powerfully entered his life. Brian experienced God-given, supernatural visitations following his conversion, and he joined a local church. He was mentored as a new believer by a pastor who truly cared for him. Shortly after, he married a lovely young lady he met in church. They had a family together and he delighted in his new life in Christ, saying that he had never been happier.

Five years into their marriage, he planted a church. His congregation honored and exalted him as a mighty man of God. His church quickly grew to a couple of thousand members, and he expanded his ministry to national television. Young women in the church started showing him attention and affection. Congregation members often gave him extravagant personal gifts, business and vacation opportunities and large amounts of money. He aligned himself with business owners and city government leaders, befriending them in order to obtain their favor and public endorsement for his increasing sphere of influence. Within the first three years of his initial church plant, he was leading a church of over 5,000 people and had built a building that held 7,000. In the next few years, the church was bursting at the seams with four services every Sunday and over 12,000 members.

Over the years the growing demands of his church and ministry took a toll on his marriage, and he decided that he deserved better. Why should he live in an uncomfortable marriage when he had lost his fresh love for his wife and "the cream of the crop" was readily available to him? Why should he give his wife the time of day when she was not 100% in support of his ministry anyway? Why should he care about her when she was not giving him what he needed or wanted? Why should he put up with that kind of tension in his life?

Brian's children were his public trophies. They were intelligent, well-behaved, attractive and well groomed. He introduced his wife and children every Sunday morning in church, having them stand, smile and wave to the church members. He would honor them in public in order to impress the congregation by painting the picture of the model family, but it was all for show. Behind the scenes he emotionally abused and neglected both his wife and his children.

Everything in Brian's life was about him. He lied, flirted with young women in the church, watched pornography on the internet, went on drinking sprees and spent church money inappropriately on personal pleasures. He openly preached against such things but privately considered himself an exception to the rule. He loved his ministry and the attention it gave him. He put "yes men" around himself and operated in control and manipulation to achieve his agendas. His anointing and the ministry of the Spirit and the Word were authentic, but his motives in ministry and his personal life were about fulfilling his own pleasures.

His son was 12 and his daughter 10 when Brian was

publicly exposed for having an affair with a beautiful young woman who worked as his personal assistant. The media had a heyday exposing his antics and hypocrisy. His family and the church were devastated. When he was caught there was no true remorse, only feigned. After all, he had become the master at giving people what they expected. Before the public he shed remorseful tears and appeared humbled and broken, but justified his actions saying that his wife was falling short of giving him what he needed. Nothing in his world was ever truly his fault. He shared privately with his church board that his wife would often lose her temper, swear at him and had thrown objects at him while in a rage. He concluded, "No man of God needs to put up with this. I deserve better and I am going to have better. Any man in my situation would have done the same thing." They tried to convince him to work out the problems in his marriage and to think of his children, but he refused. He emphatically stated, "I have been miserable in this marriage for years and now it is time for me to be happy." When they questioned his wife, they learned she had suffered years of emotional abuse and neglect. She admitted to losing her temper and with hesitation confessed that she felt harassed, pressured and controlled to a point where she would "lose it."

The church board made him step down from his pastorate due to his moral failure, his lack of true repentance, and his refusal to walk through normal restoration processes. He was very angry with them and took them to court to contend for his rights to the church building that he raised money for. He demanded a large severance. He won the court battle and received a generous settlement in his favor. He filed for divorce from his wife. Although she contested the divorce as she wanted to work things out, he was awarded it. He gave her custody of the children with visitation privileges and agreed to pay the minimum support required by law for the maintenance of his wife and children.

Brian moved to a different state to start a new life. He had pushed his divorce through quickly, and the moment it was official he eloped with his lover. He bought himself and his new wife a new home, with all the furnishings, from his severance and the court settlement.

Through his disregard to pay the alimony and child support, his ex-wife lost the house in twenty months because of financial pressures. She sought legal counsel to attempt to enforce the payments but it became too emotionally taxing for her. Others stepped in to help her but it was too late to rescue the house. Eventually he was legally forced to make payments. He seldom called or visited his children. When he did, he spent large amounts of money on them, lavished them with gifts and told them how much he loved them. He often publicly testified of how much he loved his children and how much he blessed them.

His family and his local church were shipwrecked. In the midst of it Brian boasted to personal friends that he had never been happier. One concerned board member said to him, "Don't you care about all the people you have hurt?" He responded, "Yeah, but they will get over it. They have to forgive me. I'm hurting, too, because of the way they have treated me." It was all about Brian.

Brian used his charisma, faith and magnetic personality to build another large congregation within one year of his divorce and re-marriage. After four years, Brian was once again disillusioned with his wife and the confinements that their new baby brought to his ministry and life. The old patterns were in motion again.

Brian died suddenly of a heart attack at age 41. He left behind two devastated and destroyed families and two devastated churches.

A spirit of narcissism deceived Brian.

Jessica

Jessica was a 32-year-old single woman and a successful executive in an advertising firm. She had won numerous awards for her performance in the company and she had become close to Doug, the company's CEO. Doug was 48 years of age and happily married to his wife of 22 years. He had two college-age children who were the pride of his life. He would often talk about his wife and children. His office was full of framed photos and he was a good family man, successful in his endeavors.

Jessica envied his wife and was eaten up with desire to have Doug for herself. She would sometimes by the hour imagine schemes to capture his heart, and made it her goal to become "his woman." This was not the first time Jessica had ruined a marriage. Eventually her seductions and manipulations drew his heart and an emotional affair developed between them.

Doug was often confused and wavered, determining to pull out of the relationship, but Jessica would always convince him that they were made for each other. One weekend while attending a convention in another city, Jessica invited him to her hotel room to talk over some business strategies. After having a few drinks they tragically ended up in a sexual relationship.

Doug came to the realization of what he had done and felt deep remorse. He attempted to cut off the relationship once and for all, but Jessica manipulated more with dramatic emotional outbursts and threats. He didn't want to hurt her so he continued in the relationship for a season until he was overcome with guilt and shame. He finally confessed to his wife and terminated the relationship. His wife was wounded beyond belief but she forgave him. They went to marriage counseling and started to rebuild the broken foundations.

Doug asked Jessica to leave the company in light of the situation. She was very angry and not willing to let go of her position. She did not care that she had deeply hurt Doug, his wife, his family and the workplace. She did not care that she had harmed a marriage. She was only concerned about herself and was very upset about her loss. One of her co-workers challenged her one day regarding her attitude and she responded, "But what about me? I have been hurt in this, too. He dumped me! How do you think I feel?" No one could convince her that she had done wrong. According to her perspective, she was the victim.

Jessica finally did leave the company and moved on, but not without a fight. She went to Human Resources and then secured an attorney. At the end of the process she sued Doug and the company and won over one million dollars. She told a friend after the court awarded her the settlement, "A million is nothing compared to what I would have gotten if he had married me. The guy is worth millions and I would have lived in luxury for life. He should have left his wife and married me. His wife is not worthy of him."

The spirit of narcissism controlled Jessica.

Gordon

Gordon worked at a high-end department store as a salesman in the shoe department. He had a base income with performance bonuses. Gordon was highly successful in sales but was unscrupulous in his tactics. He was uncaring about the effects of the manipulations and pressures he made on the clients or other salespersons in his department. Although committed to prosperity in sales, he ambitiously desired the management position, which he eventually was awarded. As a manager, Gordon failed terribly. His narcissistic agendas were obvious to the sales staff and they were not motivated to perform for him. He took all the credit for their sales and rudely pressured them when their performance was not up to his expectations. He also pressured customers when they walked away without making a purchase. Many quit his department. He was brought before the store manager and confronted concerning his shortcomings. Gordon became very defensive and went into a rage. He put demands on the store manager for more income and better staff. His selfish attitude, numerous demands, blame shifting and lack of restraint contributed to his immediate termination. Gordon was fired that day due to numerous filed complaints against him both by customers and his sales staff.

Gordon was angry when he went home that evening to his wife of four years. His wife was a hard working teacher at the local elementary school. She was a faithful wife and tried to comfort him, but he refused comfort. He was up all night pacing back and forth, rehearsing retaliation that he intended on giving to the store manager. He finally wrote him an email full of anger and demanded that he meet with him. When his wife woke up, he once again dumped on her with his angry perspective.

Later that morning, after his wife went to work, he received an email by the company's corporate management denying his request to meet with the manager. He became even angrier. However, as he looked through the classified ads in the newspaper, he noticed a seminar on business success. He signed up for it hoping that it might open doors for him. He needed something big to open up fast, as he had no savings. He always spent his money on his personal wardrobe, grooming, nicer vehicles and on the latest and greatest entertainment media.

At the business seminar, Gordon was very impressed with the presenter. He liked the vibrant dynamics he moved in, his trendy appearance, excellent physique, and was especially impacted by the testimony of his multi-million dollar business success. Throughout the seminar he envisioned himself in the presenter's shoes. He purchased the $2,500 success motivation training DVDs with his wife's credit card. He immediately went into his home office, locked the door and began watching the DVDs by the hour. When his wife asked him to come out and join her for dinner, he opened the door with his eyes glazed over and said, "Do not disturb me. I am going to be a very successful businessman making millions of dollars every year." He locked himself in the room day after day, preparing for the millions. After a week or two, he informed his wife that he was going to start a business, but he needed her financial help. She explained to him that she already needed to make extra money to pay off the $2,500 expense for the DVDs, as well as all the household bills. He convinced her to sign for a loan for his business' start up. He informed her that he was going to teach success motivation seminars and make thousands of dollars every week. He also informed her that he was going to create a product of his teachings (that were based on what he learned through the DVDs) as well as film an infomercial where he could make millions by selling the product and by advertising his seminars.

His wife was completely opposed to his business plan and explained that he did not have enough experience and success in business to be able to teach it yet. His eyes glassed over and he glared at her with his finger pointed in her face, saying, "Don't you ever question my ability to perform. I am called to do this and I will do it. I am going to apply for a $150,000 line of credit on the house and you WILL sign for it. You will not hold me back!"

Through pressure, his wife consented to sign for the line of credit. He sold his car and bought a higher end one, and spent $15,000 on a new wardrobe. He paid a graphic designer to brand his new endeavor, paid for advertising and marketing, rented a hotel conference room and hired a producer for the infomercial. He quickly absorbed the $150,000 and also maxed out their credit cards.

Every aspect of his plan was an absolute flop. His inexperience was obvious to *all three* participants in his seminar, and to the producer of the infomercial. He was offended with the instructions of the director, and fired him halfway through, deciding to direct himself, telling the camera personnel what to do in order to get the best shot of him.

When he pitched his infomercial to television stations, they were appalled at the "cheesiness" of the production, and he received one rejection letter after another. He was finally accepted by an obscure station in a small region of the USA that was willing to broadcast him at 3 a.m. at a budget rate of $25,000 an hour. He had the misconception that stations would pay him to air the program. He had no budget left for airtime and was left at a standstill.

Gordon would not admit to his mistakes and tension developed in the marriage. He made demands on his wife to work extra jobs in order to support the household needs and his debt. He hid himself in his study, watching DVDs of successful businessmen, and he watched infomercials on television networks, dreaming of the day when he would make his millions.

His wife invited a pastor over to speak into Gordon's life, but it only made him angry. After the pastor left he yelled at his wife, accusing her of not supporting him. Gordon continued to emotionally abuse her. One night he came home from watching a movie and found a note from his wife saying she couldn't take it any longer and had decided to leave him. Gordon was angry and wanted sympathy but none of their friends would agree with him. They pleaded with him to get some help, but he refused. He blamed his wife for his failure. He blamed the church for not supporting his choices. He pointed his finger at everyone but himself.

Over the next three years, his wife returned twice to give the marriage another try. Each time she was met with more abuse. She finally left for good and moved to another part of the country to start a new life. Gordon put so much emotional pressure on her that she made a decision to take nothing with her. All their furniture and belongings were left with Gordon. He lost the house and blamed the economy. After losing the house, he sold all the furniture and lived in the back of his car for months. Gordon was alone. No one could speak sense into him. He was unteachable, unreachable.

A spirit of narcissism blinded and controlled Gordon.

Narcissism in the Church

There are many wonderful, humble and self-sacrificing leaders in the body of Christ. They are true servants who love the Lord and minister to His people with grace and humility. Most of the leaders I know are definitely of that heart and posture. However, the spirit of narcissism can tempt and control those in the body who are ignorant of the enemy's devices and who do not guard their hearts. Leaders can be susceptible to this spirit due to the celebrity profile and handling that is expected and demanded by some.

Pastors or evangelists who are bound by narcissism are often very charismatic leaders who have magnetic personalities. They love the limelight and demand special attention, including monetary extravagance, often in the name of "honor." They may have grown up in a troubled, abusive or neglected home life or childhood. Through ignorance, or pride, they may not have allowed the Holy Spirit the freedom to heal them completely. Unteachable, unreachable and prideful, the narcissistic leader can confuse, numb and deceive others into thinking they are invincible, anointed, powerful and deserving of "superstar" treatment. Those who work for them or who follow them are often deceived and controlled by deceptive mindsets and teachings that fortify the leader's self idolatry. In extreme cases, you find examples such as cult leader Jim Jones, who in 1978 led over 900 of his followers to their death through a mass suicide.

Unresolved narcissistic behaviors in a leader can have a variety of effects on his/her followers or congregation. This leader mentors and clones other leaders that mirror the leader's self-centered personality and deception. The narcissist patterns are both taught and caught, and thus transferred to others.

A leader who is bound by this spirit needs rescue. And so do their followers. We must be discerning, awake, and sensitive to the Holy Spirit. Our discernment must never cross a line and turn to bitter judgment and criticism. Unconditional love that knows healthy boundaries and the power of fervent and relentless prayer can work glorious miracles of freedom.

> I urge, then, then, first of all, that requests, prayers, intercession and thanksgiving be made for everyone – for kings and all those in authority, that we may live peaceful and quiet lives in all godliness and holiness. This is good, and pleases God our Savior, who wants all men to be saved and to come to a knowledge of the truth (1 Timothy 2:1-4 NIV).

> Greater love has no one than this, that one lay down his life for his friends. You are My friends if you do what I command you (John 15:13-14).

Not only *leaders* in the church are susceptible to a narcissistic spirit. I know many pastors and overseers who have been emotionally and spiritually devastated when one narcissistic individual in the church or ministry pressured them with relentless demands and needs. They eventually turned members of the congregation against the leader or other members of the church. Individuals bound by narcissistic spirits have been known to destroy entire churches, ministries, and leaders.

CHAPTER THREE

Overcoming Narcissism

Whether you suffer with the actual disorder, a demonic bondage, or even simple symptoms of narcissistic behavior – ***narcissism can be overcome!*** If you have a desire to be free, you can be. All things are possible, only believe. *"So if the Son makes you free, You will be free indeed"* (John 8:36). *"You will know the truth, and the truth will make you free"* (John 8:32). The Bible gives clear instruction on how to overcome narcissism.

Admit You Need Help – Honest Evaluation

Until an individual recognizes their need for help, they will not be able to come free. Because of the nature of the deception involved in narcissistic behavior, an intervention is almost always needed. In an intervention, concerned family members, friends or co-workers will sit down and lovingly and skillfully confront their specific concerns identifying the narcissistic patterns. The persons involved in intervention must have genuine, deep care for the narcissist. They also need the maturity to establish boundaries and to resist the rejection, blame and retaliation that will most likely be directed at them at some point during or following the intervention. They must be discerning and able to withstand manipulation. Getting a narcissist to see their need for help is absolutely essential to freedom. It is a challenging assignment and needs much prayer, but all things are possible.

> But He gives a greater grace. Therefore it says, "God is opposed to the proud, but gives grace to the humble" (James 4:6).

True, Heartfelt Repentance

The narcissist must take ownership for their actions and motivations and be willing to sincerely repent. Repentance involves admission of a wrong and the willingness to turn away from it. They must confess their sins associated with narcissism, repent, and receive forgiveness. True repentance is the foundation for freedom.

Narcissism hurts others. It is important for a narcissist to seriously take ownership of how they have hurt others. Making a list of the people they have hurt and the ways they have hurt them is beneficial. The Holy Spirit is able to bring things to their mind. After the list is complete, they should ask the Lord to forgive them and also ask for forgiveness to those they have hurt. It may also be necessary to make restitution.

Die to Self

Jesus taught us to deny ourselves, take up our cross daily and follow Him (Luke 9:23).

If you are bound by narcissism, there is only one way to receive complete deliverance and that is to die – "die to self." In the myth, Narcissus was unable to overcome no matter who tried to help, comfort or console. He finally died at the side of the pond. In that place of death, a beautiful flower came forth.

Jesus offers us freedom through His death on the cross. We are taught in Scripture to reckon ourselves dead to sin. We are to see ourselves "crucified with Christ" as we identify with His death. We cannot experience resurrection into the new life of Christ until we embrace death to self. The cross came before resurrection. The sins of selfishness, self-absorption, self-exaltation and self-focus can all be dealt with through the power of the cross. They were nailed to the cross in Christ two thousand years ago. The cross is an instrument of death.

When we die to ourselves we are then free to live to serve others and to love others. A dead person is unable to act selfishly, get offended or walk in pride. We are to reckon ourselves dead to sin and alive to God. Like Jesus, we choose to deny ourselves and live for the benefit of others. "Unless a grain of wheat falls into the earth and dies, it remains alone; but if it dies, it bears much fruit" (John 12:24). In the myth, the beautiful flower did not come forth until Narcissus died.

> But he that is greatest among you shall be your servant. And whosoever shall exalt himself shall be abased; and he that shall humble himself shall be exalted (Matthew 23:11-12 KJV).

Deal with the Roots

Where there is bad fruit there is a bad root. The root(s) need to be identified and dealt with.

1. Generational iniquity. The Bible states that the sins of the parents are visited on the children to the third and fourth generations (Exodus 20:5). It is possible for sins associated with narcissism, such as self-centeredness, self-idolatry and pride, to be passed down through the generation line in the same way physical weaknesses are sometimes passed down from one generation to another. Deliverance from narcissism can be experienced when we identify generational roots, forgive our forefathers and by faith cut off the generational transference.[1]

[1]The transference of the attitudes and behavior can be transmitted from a narcissist to others through: (1) generational iniquitous strongholds; (2) taught behavior through official teaching of mindsets (i.e., a sales manager teaching his sales staff selfish motivational strategies); (3) living in the environment of narcissistic attitudes and "catching" the behavior.

2. Childhood rejection, abuse and/or r The onset of narcissism is usually in infancy, chil and early adolescence. The first five years of a child's life are extremely important in their emotional and behavioral development. If a child is rejected, neglected or emotionally, verbally, physically or sexually abused, the effects of it could create an established foundation of brokenness in the inner heart. That broken, bruised and empty place longs to be whole. We were not created to be rejected or mistreated, but loved and accepted. When true love and acceptance are not shown to a child, then vulnerability to responses such as self-focus and self-absorption can set them up for narcissistic patterns. A child does not know how to rightly discern these issues. They just know they feel empty and bad inside and want to feel good. This empty, rejected, neglected or abused place within is a landing strip for narcissism. That place in their heart will always demand to be satisfied with things that will make them feel good.

Identifying the wounds of childhood rejection, neglect and abuse are an important part of freedom. Once they are identified, the one bound by narcissism can forgive those who hurt them, receive healing for the wounds and break off the spiritual assignments of the enemy. There are many books written and courses taught on the subject of healing childhood wounds and the process of inner healing. I suggest the teachings of John and Paula Sanford. The first book in their

Transformation Series, *Transformation of the Inner Man,* is excellent.

Good godly counseling, inner healing and deliverance are important processes in healing these wounds.

3. Taught behavior patterns. If a person lives in an atmosphere of narcissistic behavior, they can easily learn to respond in like manner through constant example. Living or working in a narcissistic environment can be a set up for transference.

A woman named Ingrid grew up in a home where her parents were very focused and aggressive in their business. She often observed her parents compromise the well-being of others in order to establish advantages for themselves. They would boast about their antics openly with their children and teach them things like, "If you are going to be successful, then you have to do what you have to do. The strong one wins!" Her parents mocked the people they took advantage of in front of their children. Ingrid remembers her father saying, "They were idiots to fall for that plan. How stupid can you get? They deserve to lose their investment!" Then he laughed.

They would take their earnings and buy better cars, furniture, take the children on exotic vacations and always boast in the fact that they "deserved the high life." They would also compare themselves with others in front of the children, saying things like, "Our family is much more successful than everyone else living on this block!" Ingrid grew up in an environment of narcissism and learned to do whatever it took to make herself happy and successful. She learned to manipulate, take advantage of, deceive and seduce in order to get her way. She learned the behavior.

When an adverse behavior is learned, it is important to recognize it, repent, get into healthy environments and relationships, and learn new patterns. This takes time to establish.

4. Celebrity treatment. When someone is constantly exalted and treated preferentially, they can come to believe that the world revolves around them. A minister once shared how they were taught in Bible school to keep a distance between themselves and the congregation. They were also taught that as a leader of the church they were "The Man of God" and deserved the double honor of the congregation. Of course, believers are to honor those who serve in leadership, but this situation got out of hand. He became an object of worship in his congregation. People were taught to give extravagant financial gifts to "The Man of God" in order to honor him, and were shunned if they didn't. He had a security squad around him to keep people from getting close.The church hired a chauffeur, personal tailor and chef for him. He treated all who worked for him with a condescending attitude and expected them to work for a low income as a "holy sacrifice." He taught them that it was a divine blessing for them to serve "God's anointed servant." He, on the other hand, demanded an excessively large salary, with perks! After all, he was "The Man of God." His belief was that everyone existed in his life to bless him, "The Mighty Man of Faith." He had a very high opinion of himself. He was a gifted leader but he demanded celebrity treatment from those who were in his realm of influence. This VIP treatment and expectation became the root of his narcissistic behavior.

After a family tragedy, a nasty division in the church and a major investment collapse, he sought counsel and discovered the patterns of narcissism that had formed as a result of his church "culture." He was greatly humbled through this series of tragic events and was set free from the deceptive mindsets of narcissism.

Sometimes, a celebrity mindset is developed in childhood. A young boy named Caleb was a "child genius." He had a very high IQ and was nicknamed "The Whiz-Kid." His parents entered him into many contests and he even appeared on some television programs. He won every contest and tournament. His home was filled with trophies and certificates. He was granted cash prizes and scholarships.

His family, friends and tutors treated him like a celebrity from a young age. He was the central focus for the family, and life evolved around his gift. His name and photograph were on posters, websites and announcement media. He grew up with a self-centered attitude. Whatever he demanded, he got. His every wish was his parent's command. He manifested narcissistic behavior from a young age and, unfortunately, he never grew out of it. At 17 years of age, he had a psychotic episode and his world collapsed around him. He was hospitalized, medicated and treated for the disorder, but never recovered. He could no longer concentrate on his academics, and his mind lacked sharpness due to the medication. The focus was still on him, but it was the kind of attention he did not want. Local journalists wrote about the health problem in the newspapers and one morning he read the headlines of the newspaper: LOCAL GENIUS HAS LOST HIS MIND. The article was compassionate, sharing how he had been hospitalized for the health challenge, but the headline was cruel. He was devastated and lost hope. Caleb never recovered and committed suicide at age 21.

Follow Jesus

Jesus sets such an amazing example for us. Oh, to be like Him! When we follow His ways, His words and His examples, there will be no room left for narcissistic behavior. The old hymn states, "I have decided to follow Jesus, no turning back, no turning back." Turning to Jesus completely, with a whole heart, and following

His example of love and righteousness, will truly bring about the fruit of freedom. Psalm 23 promises that our *Good Shepherd will lead us in paths of righteousness for His name's sake*. He will never lead us astray.

Move in the Opposite Spirit

Moving in the opposite spirit is a great warfare strategy in the Kingdom. Narcissism is based on selfishness, therefore death to self is the answer for victory. Narcissism is full of pride. Therefore, walking in humility is the greatest weapon against it. Narcissism is self-absorbed, therefore look for ways to be attentive to the needs of others and sow blessings into their lives in order to sincerely encourage them. If you take each and every symptom of narcissism and find the opposite behavior, you ***will*** find the heart of God.

Renew the Mind

I enjoy making decrees of the Word of God every day. It is very powerful because the Word both washes and renews the mind. We are what we think, so it is important to align our thoughts with God's thoughts. God is void of all narcissistic beliefs. He is perfect and just in all His ways. As you read and proclaim the Word of God each day, your mind will be washed and renewed. Playing Bible CDs throughout your day and even while you sleep is also beneficial. Years ago

I wrote a little booklet called *Decree*, a helpful tool for empowering believers. I continue to use that booklet to this very day.

The battlefield is in the mind and therefore Paul taught:

> For though we walk in the flesh, we do not war according to the flesh, for the weapons of our warfare are not of the flesh, but divinely powerful for the destruction of fortresses. We are destroying speculations and every lofty thing raised up against the knowledge of God, and we are taking every thought captive to the obedience of Christ, and we are ready to punish all disobedience, whenever your obedience is complete (2 Corinthians 10:3-6).

Cast Out Evil Spirits Associated with Narcissism

Jesus declared that *signs would follow those who believe*, and one of those signs was the casting out of demons (see Mark 16:17). His commission to preach the Kingdom in Matthew 10:8 also included the casting out of demons. It is possible to cast them out of ourselves if we are believers in Christ. If you are not yet a born-again Christian, but you believe that Jesus is Lord and you desire Him to be your God and Savior, then simply invite

Him to come into your heart, forgive your sins and give you new life. Feel free to pray the following prayer:

Dear Lord Jesus,

I believe that You are the Son of God

and that You died on the cross for my sins.

I want You alone to be my God and Savior.

Please come into my heart and forgive all my sins.

Make me a brand new creation in You

and write my name in Your book of life.

Thank You, Jesus, AMEN.

When you pray that prayer with sincere faith, Jesus will come into your life. He is now your God and Savior. You might feel His presence or you might not. Feeling is not the testing agent; your faith is. If you believe, then He is in you. He loves you! Your new life begins. He will transform you with His love and grace from the inside out.

With Christ now in your life, if you sense a controlling force in you that causes you to feel powerless to overcome, it is possible that an evil spirit might be controlling you. Do not be afraid. Simply cast it out like Jesus taught. Command every spirit of pride, selfishness, self-idolatry, self-absorption, narcissism and any others that you might discern, to come out in the name of Jesus. Command them to come out quietly. After you make the command in Jesus' name, believe that they have left. Sometimes it helps to expel them through the natural breath. Remember, *"Greater is He who is in you than he who is in the world"* (1 John 4:4). Wickedness is no match for righteousness. Jesus is the King of kings and no power can resist Him. For more in-depth teaching and ministry on deliverance, order my *School of Deliverance* CD set and study guide.

Be Filled with the Holy Spirit

Invite the Holy Spirit to fill you with His presence and power. He is so wonderful and will fill you with His divine nature. When you are filled and overflowing with the Holy Spirit, there is no room for the enemy or for bad thoughts and behavior patterns. Be filled continually. Throughout your day invite the Holy Spirit to come and fill you with power afresh. Whenever you feel weak, remember that He is strong. Receive His strength by faith.

Resource items that will help you grow (more information in the back pages of this book):

Decree book

Decree CD

The Spiritual Cleanse CD

School of Deliverance CD set

School of Deliverance study guide

Encountering the Sevenfold Spirit of God
CD set and manual

Tongues CD

God Loves You with an Everlasting Love booklet

CHAPTER FOUR

NARCISSISM IN RELATIONSHIPS

It is very challenging to engage in a relationship with someone who is narcissistic in their behavior. Relationships are to be founded on godly love, honor and respect for each other. The exchange is to be mutual. Individuals bound by narcissism most often relate with others for the benefit of themselves. They cannot reciprocate love unless the results will bring them personal fulfillment or satisfaction.

As a result, people who are in a relationship with a narcissist will constantly suffer frustration, rejection, guilt, and shame. They often find themselves engaged in dysfunctional dynamics within the relationship. They are frequently motivated to please the narcissist in order to make them happy, keep the peace or to gain their love and acceptance. I have known those in relationship with a narcissist to even lie on behalf of the narcissist in order to gain their approval.

Friendship with a narcissist is usually shallow, one-sided, unfulfilling and aggravating. Often individuals will be attracted to a narcissist due to their popularity and charismatic personality, but the relationship will always turn to that which supports the narcissist's needs for affirmation, attention, endorsement and association. If the personal benefit to the narcissist wanes in a friendship, the relationship usually is terminated or placed at arms length by the narcissist.

A narcissist in the workplace or in a ministry position is normally extremely challenging and possibly even disastrous due to the self-absorbed and self-exalting motivation. They never labor with a pure motive to bless and encourage others unless it helps their agenda for success, increase, popularity or promotion. They can be competitive, prone to jealousy, ostentatious and often create strife in the workplace or ministry due to selfish agendas. Most of the time an individual struggling with narcissism is not teachable, and they resist discipline even if they seem to be in agreement outwardly. They beat to the sound of their own drum.

Being married to a person with narcissistic behavior is disappointing, unfulfilling, painful and often emotionally abusive. The spouse of a narcissist often lives with rejection, grueling demands and lack of attention. Some narcissists are very possessive and jealous of their spouses and therefore they control, emotionally manipulate and dominate them through shame

and blame while using them as showpieces t
their own image. A narcissist will always neec
themselves – more material things, more love, more attention, more praise, more time for themselves, more preferential treatment and more help. None of these will be enough, unfortunately. They seldom think of or care about the needs of their spouse unless it enhances their image or benefits them in some way.

The spouse of a narcissist can easily fall into dysfunction and often believe that if they just did a little bit more, performed a little bit better, were a little better looking or gave increased measures of affirmation and support, then perhaps their spouse would reciprocate their love, bringing peace and harmony into the marriage. A narcissist is unable to reciprocate with pure motives and they are never satisfied for long. As a result, the spouse faces constant disappointment, frustration, rejection, remorse and at times even abuse. Even though 75% of those diagnosed with NPD are male, females can also be affected. Both husbands and wives can be narcissistic. The following list of behavior patterns are oftentimes found in a narcissistic spouse:

1. Acts out in verbally aggressive behaviors
2. When confronted or opposed, places blame or shame, accuses
3. Is insensitive to the needs of their spouse – the world revolves around them

4. Is controlling and manipulating
5. Shows rage or outbursts of anger when their spouse disagrees with them, or makes them look bad in front of others
6. Often spends outside their budget, depends financially on their spouse, and asks for the spouse to help fund things for them. If the spouse withholds, they get upset and are often accusative and enraged. The opposite is also true for some. They are the breadwinners for the family but withhold finance from their spouse and use the household funds for their own goals, purposes, and pleasures.
7. Talks about themselves constantly and seldom seem interested in the life, needs or interests of their spouse
8. Expects special treatment from their spouse
9. Very sensitive if they are insulted even in the most subtle way (spouses usually feel like they are walking on thin ice and must be careful how they word things or voice complaints)
10. Shows one side of their personality in public but another side in private (they are hypocritical and can go out of their way to impress people)
11. Spouse can feel emotionally battered and confused

12. Spouses' self esteem can diminish over time

LIVING WITH A NARCISSIST

While reading this book, it is possible you may recognize someone you know, perhaps even someone you live with, who manifests the symptoms of narcissism. Living with a narcissist can be extremely complex, as they desire to be loved and yet reject the one who loves them. They are incapable of truly loving others when bound by this spirit and mindset. It is difficult to live with the manipulations, deceptions, control, selfishness, and self-focus that are very much a part of the narcissistic person. The following are some points that might help encourage you. Remember that all things are possible when you believe in Jesus!

Do not blame yourself. A narcissist is unable to truly love. No matter how hard you try, it will never be enough. Their demands will never be satisfied. It is not your fault. Do not take responsibility for their shortcomings and behavior. Do **not** blame yourself.

Establish boundaries. A narcissist can make enormous demands on the emotions, time and gifts of those near to them. Do not be intimidated and pressured. Do not be afraid to say *no*. Establish your boundaries. Do not allow abusive assaults against your emotions, body, or sexuality in any way. If needed, share carefully with someone you trust, bringing the situation into the light in order to receive counsel and support.

There are times when individuals must give themselves some space and distance from the narcissist. A woman named Tina worked for a boss who was very narcissistic. She addressed his negative and demeaning comments towards her a number of times but he never apologized, or even tried to change. In fact, when she addressed them, he would get angry and turn the blame back on her. These responses always confused her.

After many failed attempts to set boundaries, she had a heart-to-heart talk with him regarding the effect his words and behavior were having on her and others. He showed no remorse, and in fact he retaliated. He did not respect her boundaries or requests. Tina was confused and hurt but unwilling to live in such an atmosphere, so she resigned. She loved her job but did not want to allow the abuse, injustice and manipulation of her boss to affect her life at the workplace. She established her boundaries.

Love. Ultimately the power of true love will set the narcissist free if they are willing to receive it. True love, however, needs to be tough, confrontational and extremely honest at times. A strong commitment to love unconditionally will give you the grace to endure.

Forgiveness is an important part of love. I once ministered to a young woman whose husband had cheated on her. I shared with her about the power of forgiveness. She replied, "If I forgive him, I will be letting him off the hook." I responded and said, "No, my dear, you will be getting his hook out of you." Unforgiveness, bitterness and offense will affect your health and well-being. We must forgive ... and forgive ... and forgive. You might not feel it, but you can choose it.

A young Christian woman I know lives in mid-America with a narcissistic husband. She became aware of his struggles through rude awakenings early in their marriage and since has believed God for his freedom. It has not been an easy journey. She established in her heart a strong, non-negotiable love covenant with her husband before God. Love always wants the best for the sake of another. Sometimes the best is not satisfying their every wish, or facilitating and/or covering inappropriate behavior. She learned to be loving, caring, kind, giving and gentle, yet confrontational when needed. She maintains strong boundaries.

From time to time, when her husband's responses were emotionally abusive, she would leave the home for a few days.One time she left for a few weeks in order to establish her boundaries and get re-empowered in love. On that occasion, she spent time praying for more grace, more love and more wisdom. She spoke to her husband over the phone and helped him reason through the situation while maintaining her clear position. She endeavored to help him see through a different lens. She never gave up and some change has come as a result.

Love never fails. Living with a narcissist will test your love and patience. If you pass the tests you will carry a strong authority and anointing in the essence, reality and power of love.

In the 1991 Walt Disney movie, "Beauty and the Beast," we see a prime example of narcissistic behavior.

The Beast was selfishly in love with himself at the exclusion of the welfare and happiness of others. Because of the curse that was put on him he must love (and be loved in return) or he would remain a Beast forever. Being a narcissist, he could not love completely. But with the pure and unselfish love of another (Belle, who was unaware of her own beauty) the Beast was set free to be the Prince again. Not only would he now love (and be loved) completely, but his own appearance even transformed back to his original self.

Faith. All things are possible, only believe. Stand on the promises of God and believe for the Lord's intervention and deliverance with unwavering faith. Ultimately, each individual has a free will, but the Lord's grace is amazing. Never, never, never give up! A woman left her husband due to the abuse of narcissistic behavior but she never stopped believing for his healing. To this day, there has been no evidence of change but she is still standing in faith for her ex-husband's deliverance from narcissism. She has moved on with her life but is determined to never give up. She quietly and confidently stands in faith for his freedom.

Reward. Sometimes living with a narcissist can seem unbearable and constantly challenging. You must posture yourself to receive everything you need from the Lord. A narcissist is incapable of loving until they are set free. Therefore, you must receive your love directly from the Lord. A narcissist is unable to truly give encouragement unless it benefits them in some way, so you must receive your encouragement directly from the Lord. As you draw close to the Lord, you will be granted everything you need to live a good life. He IS your life! He is the One who will empower you, fulfill you and strengthen you. Isaiah 61:7 in *The Message* Bible says, "Because you got a double dose of trouble and more than your share of contempt, your inheritance in the land will be doubled and your joy goes on forever." Receive your reward by faith. In His presence you will find the fullness of joy.

Courage. Oftentimes people fear the narcissist due to their unpredictable rages, retaliations, and shame and blame techniques. God is not an accuser; He is a lover. Have the courage to face the reactions of the narcissist while maintaining your peace. You are loved and cherished and must fight to maintain that belief. If the situation is abusive, you will need the courage to walk away from the abuse and receive healing. You might need courage to disclose your situation to a friend or counselor. Darkness is empowered in secret. Be courageous and bring everything into the light.

Moving on. You have a life to live. Your life is a gift to you and it doesn't have to be lived in the shadow of a narcissist. Live your life to the fullest in love, righteousness and honor. When you are filled with the Lord, knowing that all you need is found in Him, you are ready to move forward. There is a whole world out there for you to both impact and enjoy. You might feel called to remain in a situation with an undelivered narcissist in your life, but when you are secure in the Lord, you will have everything you need to live in freedom in the midst of all the challenges you may face.

My husband and I had a prison ministry years ago. After we led prisoners to Jesus, they still were locked up in their cell at night, but they were no longer confined by that cell. They enjoyed freedom as their new life unfolded. One night when we visited, an inmate was in tears after receiving Christ. He said, "I have spent years in prison always longing for my freedom. I even attempted an escape. But since I received Christ, I have never known such great freedom. It is beyond anything I ever dreamt of. In or out of this building, I am free at last."

CHAPTER FIVE

A Final Word

In Christ, we are called more than conquerors. We are to be overcomers in this life. We are His light that expels darkness. We are the salt of the earth that preserves. The Word teaches us that nothing is too difficult for Him and that all things are possible to those who believe.

In the world we live in there are many challenges. We don't need to look far to see them. We live in an immoral and corrupt society, but there is always hope. God is looking for a remnant of people who will stand strong, fight and persevere in order to see righteousness and freedom abound. We are anointed like Jesus with the Holy Ghost and with power. Our call is to invade darkness with His light and set the captives free.

There are many who are held captive to narcissism. They are imprisoned by the deception of this wicked spirit and destructive, deceptive mindset. It is a demonic stronghold that we in Christ can and will break.

Many in these days will receive total deliverance from the grip of this spirit. We will prevail. We will win!

Imagine the body of Christ full of believers who love each other perfectly, a body that always esteems each other more than themselves, a body that is generous, kind, gentle and patient, and a people who are willing to lay down their lives for the well-being of another. Does this sound like Jesus? We are His body in the earth. This is what He is looking for.

A fire of purging is coming to the body of Christ (see Matthew 3:10-12; Isaiah 6:1-7; Malachi 3:2-3; 4:1). Everything that is not of love will be burned. Let's call for that purging fire now. Allow the dross to burn.

> Lord Jesus,
> Purge me of everything that is not of You, that is not of Your love. Send Your deliverance and Your purifying fire to every narcissistic thought, attitude, word, action and behavior pattern in my life, and in the lives of those I love. Cleanse me with the power of Your blood and forgiveness. Heal in me the things that hurt others, and make me a vessel of Your great love and power! AMEN

1 Corinthians 13

(*The Message* Bible)

Love never gives up.

Love cares more for others than for self.

Love doesn't want what it doesn't have.

Love doesn't strut,

Doesn't have a swelled head,

Doesn't force itself on others,

Isn't always "me first,"

Doesn't fly off the handle,

Doesn't keep score of the sins of others,

Doesn't revel when others grovel,

Takes pleasure in the flowering of truth,

Puts up with anything,

Trusts God always,

Always looks for the best,

Never looks back,

But keeps going to the end.

The Greatest Power...

The Greatest Weapon...

The Greatest Person...

in the entire universe...

is LOVE.

Lord, reduce us to LOVE.

Bibliography

The Holy Bible (NASB and The Message)

The Narcissism Epidemic: Living in the Age of Entitlement (book) by psychologists and professors Jean Twenge and W. Keith Campbell

Malignant Self Love – Narcissism Revisited (book) by Dr. Sam Vaknin

Online Encyclopedia Britannica

Wikipedia, the free dictionary

Genealogical Guide to Greek Mythology by Carlos Parada
Understanding the Hidden Patterns that Motivate Abusers: Narcissists, Borderlines, and Sociopaths (book) by Richard Skerritt

Other Books and Resources by Patricia King

Available at the "Store" at **XPmedia.com.**

Decree. *Decree a thing, and it shall be established (Job 22:28).* Patricia King wrote *Decree* to help believers activate the power of the Word in key areas of their lives, including blessing, favor, glory, health, provision, love, victory, wisdom, family, business, spiritual strength and others.

Decree CD. Patricia King speaks forth many of the decrees that are in the *Decree* book. Heather Clark accompanies with powerful music. When declarations of the Word are proclaimed over you, the Word is then activated to strengthen your spirit man and prepare you for every good Kingdom work.

The Spiritual Cleanse soaking CD is full of prayers and decrees written and proclaimed by Patricia King, accompanied by worship music from Steve Swanson. As you listen, you will be soaked in the purifying presence of the Living Word of God. It is like going to a spiritual spa!

Other Books and Resources by Patricia King

Available at the "Store" at **XPmedia.com.**

The School of Deliverance, 8 CD Set and Manual. Do you suffer with guilt, shame, emotional pain, addictive behavior, irrational fears or rejection? Are you trapped by past failures or generational bondage?

The School of Deliverance introduces you to realms of healing and deliverance as Patricia King teaches, preaches, and prophesies you into new-found freedom. Wounds of the past will be healed, and oppressive powers will be broken over lives. You can walk in wholeness and freedom. And you can minister it to others!

God Loves You with an Everlasting Love. This booklet by Patricia King is designed to introduce you to the greatest revelation anyone could ever receive. It is the revelation of God's unconditional love for you – the love that was perfectly tested and proven at the cross, 2,000 years ago. Drink deeply of this revelation and come to the full realization that: God Loves You with an Everlasting Love!

Other Books and Resources by Patricia King

Available at the "Store" at **XPmedia.com.**

Encountering the Sevenfold Spirit of God, 4 CD set by Patricia King. This teaching was revealed to Patricia during prayer time with the Lord. Learn all that the Holy Spirit has for us and how to access it. This teaching is an open door to more wisdom, revelation, understanding, counsel, might, reverence and anointing. Subjects dealt with include: "Who Is The Holy Spirit," "The Sevenfold Spirit of God," "The Seven Dimensions," "How To Encounter the Holy Spirit."

Tongues. Patricia King gives an in-depth teaching on the gift of tongues. This will give you both a solid biblical principle on this gift and an understanding on how to receive it!

Many more resources are available at the bookstore at **www.XPmedia.com**, including books, teaching sets in CD, DVD and MPs, music and more. Many resources are downloadable. Check them out!

PATRICIA KING

Patricia is president of both Extreme Prophetic and Christian Services Association. She has been a pioneering voice in ministry, with over 30 years of background as a Christian minister in conference speaking, prophetic service, church leadership, and television and radio appearances. Patricia has written numerous books, produced many CDs and DVDs, hosts Extreme Prophetic TV, and is the CEO of a popular online media network – XPmedia.com. Patricia's reputation in the Christian community is world-renowned.

Christian Services Association (CSA) was founded in Canada in 1973 and in the USA in 1984. It is the parent ministry of Extreme Prophetic, a 501(c)(3) founded in 2004 in Arizona. CSA/Extreme Prophetic is located in Maricopa, AZ and Kelowna, B.C. Patricia King and numerous team members equip the body of Christ in the gifts of the Spirit, prophetic ministry, intercession, and evangelism. CSA/Extreme Prophetic is called to spreading the gospel through media.

AUTHOR CONTACT INFORMATION

Extreme Prophetic/CSA
U.S. Ministry Center
P.O. Box 1017
Maricopa, AZ 85139

XP Canada Ministry Center
3054 Springfield Road
Kelowna, B.C VIX 1A5
CANADA

Telephone: 1-250-765-9286

E-mail: info@XPmedia.com

www.XPpublishing.com

A Ministry of Patricia King and

Christian Services Association